SANCTIFICUM

Also by Chris Abani

Sanctificum

CHRIS ABANI

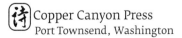 Copper Canyon Press
Port Townsend, Washington

Cover art: Victor Ekpuk, detail from *Good Morning Sunrise*, 2004. Acrylic on canvas, 48 × 48 inches.

Copper Canyon Press is in residence at Fort Worden State Park in Port Townsend, Washington, under the auspices of Centrum. Centrum is a gathering place for artists and creative thinkers from around the world, students of all ages and backgrounds, and audiences seeking extraordinary cultural enrichment.

ACKNOWLEDGMENTS

Some of these poems have appeared in *Blackbird, Bombay Gin, Court Green, diode, Farafina, Narrative, Redivider, The Southern Review,* and *Tarpaulin Sky.*

Thanks to Sarah Valentine, Peter Orner, Cristina García, Matthew Shenoda, A. Van Jordan, Patty Paine, Junot Díaz, Kwame Dawes, and Michael Wiegers.

LIBRARY OF CONGRESS CATALOGING-IN-PUBLICATION DATA

Abani, Christopher.
Sanctificum / Chris Abani.
   p.   cm.
ISBN 978-1-55659-316-1 (pbk.: alk. paper)
1. Title.
PR9387.9.A23S26 2010
821'.914 — dc22

2009043650

9 8 7 6 5 4 3 2 FIRST PRINTING

COPPER CANYON PRESS
Post Office Box 271
Port Townsend, Washington 98368

www.coppercanyonpress.org

For
Daphne

Anything beautiful about me was a gift from you.
I will see you in dreams and words.

Also, of course,
Sarah

Sanctificum (Latin): sanctify, make holy

Every true poet is a monster

TOMAŽ ŠALAMUN

Terror is a state of complete understanding

LARRY LEVIS

CONTENTS

SANCTIFICUM

Om

1

The hills of my childhood are purple with dusk and wings—
guinea fowl launched like a prayer to the still forming moon.
I hold Bean's shell to my ear. There is no sea. But only sea.
By my bed, in an empty chair, my shirt unwinds.
I remember my aunt counting the dead in the newspaper.
I never told anyone that every sliver of orange I ate
was preceded by words from high mass.
Per omnia saecula saeculorum.
Spit out pit. Amen.
Juice. Amen. Flesh.

2

A full moon leaning on a skyscraper. The taste:
qat and sweets on a tropical afternoon.
The dog's black tongue was more terrifying than its teeth.
The gravestone rising out of the puddle was more sinister
than the body we discovered as children swinging
in the summer-hot orchard.

3

The old woman singing a dirge has a voice of dust.
Sorrow lodged like a splintered bullet next to the heart.
A man once asked me in the street:
Do you own your own bones?
She likes the home I come in, I say to Cristina
as we drive toward the Golden Gate.
Bean, I repeat.
She loves the home I come in
and I am alive with fire and scars.
Here is my body, I say, eat it, do this,
remember me —

4

Even now melancholy is a skin flayed
and worn in dance through the city.
Yes, the city becomes skin too and wears me
as skin and I want to say, *This is my body,* as I stroke
the curve of the fountain in the park.
This is my blood. Drink it. Remember.
The safety of doorways is an illusion.
They lead nowhere.
This is why we build houses.
Sand, when there is no water, can ablute,
washing grain by grain even the hardest stone of sin.
But you, but you, you are a sin that I live for.
Ne Me Quitte Pas. Ne Me Quitte Pas. Ne Me Quitte Pas.
Nina's voice walks in dragging bodies,
dead black men that bled unseen in the dark
of southern nights, shaded by leaves

and the veiled eyes of hate.
And in a poem, Lucille stands in the shadow of a tree
and pours libations for our souls,
for our salt, for our gospel.

5

Somewhere a man speaks
in the dark, voice lost to rain.
I know this hunger, this need
to make patterns, to build meaning
from detritus; also the light
and the wood floor bare but for the lone slipper
tossed carelessly to one side. I admit the lies I've told.
Look, nothing has been true
since that picture of hell on the living-room wall lost its terror.
I say I want a strong woman, but unlike Neto
I cannot have the woman and the fish.
The war followed.
Children are losing their souls to the heat.
That is to say, poor American soldiers.
The rich have found a way to charge theirs to Amex.
Ask this: what is the relationship of desire to memory?
Here is a boy in the airport café, hair cropped from service.
And he closes his eyes to take a sip of coffee.
And smiles as the dark washes the desert away.

6

Los Angeles:
A red sky and angels thick like palm trees,
and garbage blown in the wind like cars
and the gluttony of SUVs
in an endless river of traffic.
Through the dark, we say, through the dark:
but do we ever really know?
There is a man in a field and he is searching for God.
Father, he says, Father.
In the distance, birds, traffic, and children.
There is a blue sky. There is a sky blue with night.
The call of the earth is a primitive song,
stomping feet and broken men.
There is a blue sky. And night.
The city is a flock of lights.
The darkness of tunnels like caves is knowledge,
also mortal. Maps are like God.
They are the city yet not the city.
They contain the city but yet do not.
We trace the lines in loss.
Sometimes we find treasure.
Sometimes something fills the mind,
something at which we pause, stopped.
The way a photograph cannot remember the living.

7

To die is to return.
To fly is to be a bird's heart.
Neither is freedom.
If it were we would have no name for it.
No language. Not even the temptation of wind
blowing a dark woman's hair away from a cliff's edge.
Instead, feathers are brought to my door every day by mystery.
Kindling for a fire, a beacon, an epiphany I cannot light.
This is the body of Christ.
Sanctificum.

Sacrament

1

Have you heard of the oracle of the Igbo?
The one called Chukwu? Just one word: God.
The oracle of God.
The voice of God.
The final arbitration.
Kpom kwem.
Deep in a grove of trees, the sacred lake,
and rising in the gloom and heat,
mist, the very breath of divinity.
The unbearable trepidation,
the worship, the sheer terror and earnestness
trembling the supplicants. And the priests
sitting on rocks and in trees on haunches,
silent like vultures or Rilke's unspeakable angels.
And then a pilgrim wades cautiously into the lake.
On the shore, the line of unannointed
shivers in a shared awe.
And if the petitioner is beautiful or strong,
the priests hold her under, then shackled,
for slavers. In the lake, red dye bubbles up
as God smacks his lips.
And that endless line of believers near faint
with the fearsome beauty of the thought:
Please consume me, God.
Consume me and find me worthy.
But don't let me die.

2

There is risk in this —
Not in the words, but the dreaded embodiment of light,
a sacred song. A river darker
than caverns immeasurable,
a sacred river; not all Ganga, not all Alph,
but still fire, still fire.
Before this flight, before this persistence
the soul is bare.
Holy the water.
Holy the smoke.
Holy the flame.
Holy, holy, holy.

3

Death is a flock of blackbirds low over muddy streets
in war-torn Sarajevo. Dirt-stained walls yearn
for all that is night. Elegies fall like raw silk.
If there is a way it is here.
Salt and ash.
This is how the Igbo clean their teeth.
Grandmother grinding charcoal
coughing as the silt rises.
Then salt rubbed into the black
as though morning were trying to temper night.
Then water and a fingertip collecting the gray,
the unidentifiable finger dipping into
a mouth held open like a wound —
A thick sludge complicates my joy.
It is made of the dissolved bones and flesh

of men we buried in swamps
behind the walls of internment. Buried
in shallow graves like a hand cupped in peat,
then bodies and lime: the hiss and sizzle, and the suck
of earth filling with water.
Of swamp digesting histories and love.
Instead of a preface, instead of a requiem,
the symphony of rain fills the night
with the distracted hurry of wild horses
crossing a plateau under a threatening sky.
I am not afraid of love, or its consequence of light,
Joy intones, chant like skin, like sand, like water.

4

There is fog this morning. On my continent
children die. African children die every day.
It's what they do.
I can still hear my mother's sewing machine
stitching the afternoon with promise. Under a tree,
in the scent of rotting fruit, I washed
bitter-leaf for dinner. Washed and squeezed.
The bitter foaming away.
Like frothy green blood from the neck of sacrifice.
A dog is barking at spirits in the heat.
Language escapes me still—see it sprinting
down the street. Crazed. A crazy man.
Babbling. Babel. This is my language.
On a wall in Sarajevo, graffiti reads:
KILLING IS MY BUSINESS
BUSINESS IS GOOD. THE FROGMAN.
Sem gave me the book with the graffiti.

In D.C. he said, My name is Sem,
eyes narrowed, even as his lips smiled.
I know this trim. A name for invisibility.
A loss for a chance to be here.
Do I not carry a pocketful of accents?
In halting speech I said it wrong: Semezdin Mehmedinović.
He smiled as though I were singing an aria.
We went back to coffee, the dark, and rain:
a Washington, D.C., street and the glow of lights.
Agi Mishol said, Choose your rebbe carefully.
Someone who sees who you can become.
I doubt there is anything like truth here in this tea shop
but the chai is good and the light on Bean is golden.

Divination

1

How can a people who have paid such a price
for life, return from the grave with such vengeance?
And who will count the Palestinian dead?
And who mourns for them? Stones and steel
and mortar bombs *will* break my bones.
In Bean's voice, Aygi returns as a girl
slender with olive in her eyes and a smile —
and snow, again snow, the cadence soft, falling.
Text message to Bean sent from my phone:
Ronald Reagan Airport.
Departure Gate—
I hope you get this.
Through night and rain and a plane.
Things wear the musk of elegy.
And maybe even a ghost. A double
rising like light from a wet road.
By an African roadside, a woman
more skeleton than flesh squats.
Death wears down her resistance.
The sun tries to be merciful.

2

I don't know why I sing
in languages I cannot understand.
Fast-moving trains draw time ahead and
then there is the sea and the blue kite of horizon;
a perfect chalice for night
and the communion sliver of moon.
I am driving to Santa Barbara.
The sun this afternoon is a fallen angel, but beautiful.
Zora said, "Black people are art."
Hallowed be thy name.
Which is to say, there is no end to ocean,
no article to limit. As for dream, he is a man
with dark robes and a gaunt face and sigh so weary
it makes the nightmare tedious. Every night he is waiting.
He doesn't think it funny when I laugh at the crow on his shoulder.
You said Mother would no longer make you sad. I believed you.
Yet over and over I wash the two dresses a woman left
after she was done with me. The smell is summer.

3

Even in the agony of waiting —
this is the way she loves the dream.
And what woke me was the scent. Like the smell
of coffee my mother beat from the folds of her day dress.
There is a small girl shivering in a stream
as her brothers keep watch from the lip of a wooden bridge,
while behind them, mere inches from their buttocks,
cars pass. Each counted in an arc of spit, each
boy puckering fast to win the count.

Their legs' kicking casually over the abyss belies their fear.
If you know sorrow, you know it hurts in the body.
I project my hope into the streets of South Africa.

       4

No I am not afraid of the eye chart:
in THE dmv
But i sHakE
at The Uniformed
COP who WaLks In.
My fear of uniforms is an old habit, comfortable.
Sometimes even the chief fryer at McDonald's can
make me break into a hot sweat if I am not expecting his glance.
Monsters don't crowd your psyche
but rather sit awkwardly on the remote control,
too polite to get up and move it, until
the constantly changing channel is unbearable.
The odds are that my political views won't stop the invasion,
but to drink Ethiopian coffee during a bomb-
storm is still rebellious.

A LETTER TO ROBERT PINSKY:

This is wood, enchanted wood.
Still the fire scorches and we say wood
still the pain burns from the club
and then we say wood
still the planks dovetail and we caress
the smooth and the rough
sensuous, delectable, and yet sorrowful
and then we say wood.

Revenant

1

Jefferson Elementary wants a name change
because Jefferson owned slaves. Sequoia
Elementary, they say. Chief
Sequoyah and the Cherokee nation owned 1,500 black slaves.
What kind of avatar cannot save a moth
from the crush of a wheelchair?
Absence births an ache.
Late at night when I can't sleep I draw plans
for the radio Christopher Leibow placed
on his father's grave.
I am unable to love my father, so this.
It is so exhausting to hate the dead.
Of course it is dangerous.
Every angel dies like this,
wings spread like rugs for God's feet.

2

Holocaust Memorial in Berlin:
Tall slabs of concrete forget what has been made.
Darkness irrigates narrow alleys between the forest
of stones. This might be a new Stonehenge.
I feel I will never escape from here.
This is knowledge, also guilt.
But the stigmata should never compare
the depths of his wounds with Christ.
Here is not the time for that.
What *is* here is a young boy picking a scab
and dabbing at the new berry of blood
with nothing more than what the moment offers.

Teenagers scream through the rows to dispel shadows.
Malinda beside me says:
You know my grandfather was in a camp in Serbia.
In the Second World War.
A work camp.
A death camp.
His ghost is here.
My breath is hot and white in the cold.
I am distracted by it.

3

A *Chicago Tribune* obituary:
In lieu of flowers, please send acerbic letters to Republicans.
In the Red Square, Lenin is sprouting fungi.
King Oedipus to the barman: She wasn't all that.

4

Someone once told me his father stole trees.

In Michele's kitchen, Yang is singing
a haunting Mongolian water song
so out of key it stops my breath.
His voice, pitted, circles the salad.

5

It does not matter how many fatwas
the Ayatollahs place on Salman,
Muhammad will always be an illiterate.
Blessings be upon his name.
But more pressing perhaps is that Gibreel,
with all that burning knowledge,
all that fire from the East, could never quite spell.

6

A buffalo drowns in a flood.
A child on a roof holds on with fatigued feet.
It might have been Burma. I can't remember.
I changed the channel.
For years I hated the Arabs with a venom.
Now I know that I cannot
blame it all on the novels of Leon Uris.
What words erase, texture resists.

Elephants

1

There was this small college in the South where I read
and three white boys in the audience
in KKK outfits, stiff like lilies for a funeral.
The walk up to them was long with fear and shame and rage.
But I took the hood off one and wore it back to the stage
and through my reading to a deafening applause.
But I mostly remember how hot it was under the fabric
and how that boy's smell filled me,
and how wet my tears were.
And Bean in the warm bed breathing softly and me cold
on the floor and writing this poem in an old notebook.
And the arrow slit of skylight lets in only a red night.
And her Gennady Aygi translations flutter by the bed
like a flock of simple white birds.
The more we promise to never leave our lovers,
the faster the horizon arrives. My lust is simpler still:
that Bean return to me every night with her gentle warmth.

2

Doesn't it always begin with a hanging?
With a moth dying against a screen door?
But what of the dreams of glory? my friends ask.
Ah, that too. But it seems there is no death
without the dying, no light without the beguiling.
Iman says a dark passageway is suitable for dance.
Shadows are the best we can do.
Even now my name startles me, reminding me of nothing.
It is hard to read the gorgeous prose of Love in the Time of Cholera
and still want to write. Sometimes it is all I can do.

And in that hotel room in Rotterdam, burning through
cigarette after cigarette and tea after tea,
a woman argues that art is the only way to be beautiful
and we agree that we are both born from the same stubborn star.
We stop arguing only once, when her husband calls
and she says to the darkness beyond the window: I miss you.
The phone cradled in the crook of her neck
as she stirs my tea. I want to cry
in the stillness of the smoke.

3

This is faith.
We are always looking into the past: even a mirror.
The you turning in a shaft of light, shirttails unfurled
like bird wings caught in the shudder of surprise.
The you so free, so full of joy. Even that you
is in the past as you see you. Even as you dance
through the motes radiating through you,
you have lost it. Yet we keep dancing.
The mended chair is already mended before we break it.

4

There is a place on the veld where elephants go to die.
Here they come across the skeletons of other elephants.
They pause amid the whiteness, raise their trunks and howl
to the absent flesh, circling the bones, picking up each one,
putting it down; circling one last time, they stand still in silence
for an age, then move. Steps less assured, slower.

Why was it so hard to tell my mother, I love you,
like the man in Sarah's translation of Gennady's poem
tracing a woman's face with a flower?
To cling to death, to a metaphor as real as a dying parent,
is to wrap language around an absence.
There are stories that can kill you.

5

It is not likely that my father and I will take a walk soon
and not just because he is dead.
But he did come back in a dream to cook
me a simple dish of beans with tomatoes
and, through the steam rising from my bowl,
he smiled as he cut me a slice of bread,
vanishing slowly with every saw.
The heart is like this sometimes.
It finds the hands of your dead father
and shaves away another layer
like a thick slab of warm bread.
Sometimes that, Tadeusz. Or sometimes this.
That the lines lead you out of the labyrinth.
That the Minotaur is your toy bear thrown casually
against a chair in the dark.
That rain will come.
That rain will come.

6

Mist rubbed from the car window smears the landscape,
and even the word, *puja,* like the hush of fallen
leaves grazing temple floors, is revolution.
For is prayer not disobedience?
The questioning of God's order?
This meter is red, the falling notes turn blue,
but what tramples them into the earth is
the turmeric of feet praying to Shiva.
This too:
smoke collecting under hair and clothes
then shaken to the dust with all the salty pleasure of sweat
and the other graces the body drops from its ocean
like pearls on a dream's string.
Is there water in the flower of a snowflake?
This precise geometry?

7

Freedom smoked a pipe on the steps of the museum
in Harare. She said, sniffing,
Winter has come early to Zimbabwe.
There was nothing gentle about this former guerrilla:
but all grace, all grace.
I didn't believe her when she said:
Once I saw butterflies like a man's soul
in a clearing, in the war. Here,
in Venice I see a gypsy singing
in St. Mark's Square. And pigeons.
Also rain and an inexplicable ray:
blue light from a stained-glass window.

This is perhaps what Freedom meant.
Wisdom met me at the airport.
It's never too far to travel home, he said.
Metaphors are everywhere.
Signs, Happiness says as the elevator stalls.
Of course they are both right.
Of course they are both wrong.

DEAR DEREK WALCOTT, PATRON SAINT OF
SHIPWRECKED POETS:

I am not Crusoe, though I may want to be.
I am a man. That much at least is not
desire. I am building a fire, a funeral pyre
for the attavus. For the ritual. I am
burning to ash in my desperate signaling.
In the distance. A fire burning and a man.

Descent

1

All those demonstrations, Mother,
of the Billings Ovulation Method;
aged seven, translating to women:
when your vulva swells,
before your period comes, insert—
and they, never meeting my eyes yet asking—
and for the virgins, the piece of a balloon stretched
over the lip of a Coca-Cola bottle was the hymen.
My mother's pen pushing against it
demonstrating pressure, pushing agonizingly,
slowly, until the virgin and I both
let our breath out in a long shuddered relief—
Like a train breaking for a tunnel.
Like the sun after a thunderstorm.
Who can say how much is remembered and how much invented?
Who can say what is right and wrong?
Countless good my mother did for those women
who didn't even know they could own
their own wombs or vaginas.
Even now, because I am a man,
this freedom is still academic.
Hail Mary full of grace—

Women in my childhood blackened their teeth with snuff.
It was said that men were drawn to that as much
as to the eloquence of their ample backsides.
Women so strong men never got
to choose anything for them.
When did these women begin to think a gentle spray
of flowers worthy of their love?
The women of my village felt their love better sated

with smoked antelope legs and baskets of bananas or yams —
children it turns out cannot eat flowers.
Yet their bodies were adorned with so much beauty.
I know they knew more than they would ever reveal to me.

2

I have seen many red nights and purple
evenings taut with cold and winterlight,
and afternoons yellow with ripe leaves,
but I have never seen the northern lights
or a comet shower or an alien or a desert crossing
from Mexico, people loping like coyotes
in the floodlight-silver night.
Although there was an evening when rounding a bend
on a river walk in London I saw a heron lift off
and slice the silence with its snakelike head,
all wings and feathers and lapping water.
A crepuscular light, brittle like a saltine, and oh, the salt.

3

Also it makes me pause to think that anyone could have
read Rilke and then engaged in the Holocaust.
When Ilya reads, the poem is wounded.
An animal crying in the face of an approaching angel
whose voice blends with its own —
Is this why Israel forgets the holocaust its people suffered
and then brings one against the Palestinians?
For Iman it is a difficult question — if we ask Israel
(and she says the name like a song, like a prayer: Is-ra-ayle)

to stop bombing the Arab, we must also condemn
the suicide bomber. For her, there is no hope for peace
as long as men measure armistice in pints of blood shed
on both sides, seeking an impossible balance.

DEAR KIMIKO HAHN:

It is not that I mean to intrude on you,
but you are the only one I can trust
not to lie to me. I must bite
deep into this feast of flesh,
no matter how disgusting,
looking for the blood beneath the blood,
skin beneath the skin.
Do you think I am a cannibal?
Worried
Chris.

Processional

1

Quench the light—
and my cousin's voice heavy
with an Igbo inflection that made it a threat,
like, "I will quench you."
Like, the man quench yesterday.
Like a fragile neck breaking.
The way our ethnicity was nearly quenched in a war
that began with a pogrom against us.
Quenched and all but gone but we raged.
Still—
Igbos littered northern streets like so many dead flowers.
I trimmed the wick. The lantern gulped hungrily for life,
stuttered once, twice, then gone.
Quenched.

And night, free at last, stirred, stretching, feral.
But I am still here so my blanket protected me,
the heat rash a reasonable price for safety.
The thing is, every day I was painted in calamine lotion
until I looked like a ghost, scaring myself as I went to bed.
And the world turns—
Once again rain, but not all water.
From the car window, winding up a snowy mountain pass
in Colorado: the frozen river looks like corroded copper,
all green and mottled white and the breath of time.
What a remarkable thing a voice is—
In Haiti the poor gather to protest in the slum Cité Soleil,
but no one is smiling at the irony.
I saw this old man once at the doctor's office;
he looked confused as though it was a mystery
why he had clung to life so savagely, so earnestly.

2

A foot poised over a pool.
The surface breaks, a boy falls in,
his laughter fills the afternoon.
Ritual is the only language we truly believe in:
tea steaming a glass mug on a table,
smoke from a cigarette filling the room with blue,
the way the sun falls across our face as we sleep.
These are our things, we say.
But somewhere a door closes and another day begins.
What if the woman we have always loved,
the one we desire to wake to, is our mother?
The holy homeless fill the city like so many weeds.
Only God's children can see them.
A blue cross on a wall is a flame.
A ball falling from the sky is a meteor.
Rust is its own kind of truth:
like blood, like cities, like sunlight on a dusty road.
We never find it, of course, but it's always there,
between the smoke and the flame.

3

This is a circle song. Like songs of old.
We go over the same territory, like a mower
religiously eating grass that will grow again.
Some call it history.
The wise say it is a pond, or river.
There are things you can only say
with a canyon. Or smoke
moving across a valley toward the mist

at the foothills. I want to return
to that boy I was, but what will I say?
What would I have him do differently?
Believe in the faith of moths?
Believe in the inevitability of shadows?
This poem is like someone waiting for a bus
so long he has lost the urge to travel.
My brothers must be as tired of this as I,
dragging love as a tally board behind us,
marking off an endless but complex math
of ego and one-upmanship and debt.
But the men who came before us didn't
teach us another way.
And even when one of us summons
the courage to break the heavy wood of it
and stoke a fire of liberation,
the others chalk up more and more.
In the end, does it really matter
who started the war?
Palestine? Israel?
Iran? Iraq?
Russia? Chechnya?
The U.S. and the rest of the world?
Break the board of death.
We are tired of tallying the wounds.

4

Beati quorum via integra est.
Cape Town, South Africa:
Rocks sunning like whales calling to cliffs
as indifferent as teeth in an octogenarian's mouth.
Dressforms in an abandoned shop haunt the night.
Note to self—Look up:
Vivant.
Revenant.
Lacunae.

5

Why would a boy who knows nothing about alchemy
and the machinations of blood and other terrors respond
to a voice calling for a rain of death and other terrors?
Red Riding Hood walks out of the forest and her basket explodes.
Count the dead spilling out of the café like rank meat thrown
to dogs in the street. Revenge begets nothing but itself.
Sometimes after a suicide bombing, flesh and bone
from the dead bomber embed themselves under
the skin of the survivors: organic shrapnel.

6

I want to speak about loss.
About my father and the word we never found.
In a dream Satan told me he was a crow
and that the small intestine was so long
God hid it in the stomach.
Perhaps this is why the death of a father
brings new life. Communion;
water and wine. Amen.
But the death of our mothers is annihilation.
There is no particular reason to believe me.

7

When has death ever been silent?
The watchword is not mute, the cry comes from the deep.
I want to go further, but I am afraid.
There are ways in which the memory of my prison
is nothing more than a scarf trailing from the hand of
a child leaning over the side of a pier, signaling
to gulls, and surf, and indifferent waves,
before being snatched by the wind.
And though I have tears, I am grateful, too.
On the boardwalk the Jimi Hendrix look-alike smiles.
This is no time for hemlock.

8

Every creation myth begins with land.
And gods plant us where we are with the help of
others that cannot be named.
I have made a talisman of my hope.
It is the glimmer of light from a house lost in the woods.
I have a cousin who walks with a shuffle.
It was cruel to think she was slow.
It is simply what circumcision does to some women.
I am looking for the words to say this.
But I remain a man, you see.
The knife is firmly in my hand.

God's Country

1

I wonder if my brother Greg remembers the throb
of the horse he rode, muscles and hair between his legs.
Or did he forget when he saw it killed for ritual,
blood spilled for love, for honor, for duty.
He was ten.
We don't talk about it.
Half-used matchbooks litter my life.
Am I afraid to lose the light?
Ask yourself, what does it mean to see only the dark?
I know what I am talking about.
After six months in a hole in the ground,
the prison is not the building, or the bars, or the beatings,
or the denials, or the lies, or the forgetting, or the negotiating—
It is the small door in your mind closing.
All cremation ovens are set to
the temperature it takes to burn the heart.
It just won't die.

2

There is no native land.
We are always on a platform
waiting for a train that almost never comes.
The express screaming through the station is a dragon.
Sometimes snow, sometimes sun. Sometimes we say,
This is my station. In truth it is all journey.
No one gives and no one takes.
The true miracle is that love happens all the time.
If there is a native land this is its geography.
I believe in God. There I said it.

This only proves I am Nigerian.
Victor had the only monkey I've met with a last name:
Mr. Modestus Tempo, Esq.
She turned out to be a girl.
This is the problem with naming.

3

Endlessly, poets lyric snow, again snow.
A glass of water on a hot day. Now there's a miracle.
"Ode to a Girl Soldier."
Look away, look away.
Mercifully the commercial always runs.
"Ode to America."
A man in Camden is dealing
leaves of grass by Whitman's house.
I am often on the wrong platform.
I am often on the opposite platform.
It is lonely here.
Those who go against the herd get eaten.
This is the way of lions and herds,
and solitary wildebeests. We follow whatever path we must.
I know a brilliant man who is more beautiful when
he sings in the shower with his girlfriend.
Love songs are a peculiar sadness.
Words can scuttle any ship. Ask Ahab.
To die is to return.
What can be said about chicken hearts left to dry
in a deep sun: brown and hard as stones?
When we say *love* we mean, I want.
When we say *sorry* we mean, forgive me.

There is little room for anyone else.
But Bean, she loves me.
How else can she keep forgiving me?

Pilgrimage

1

Nothing as definite as prayer.
A hand cups a shadow.
A heart is laid bare, open as a flower.
Somewhere between care and cacophony
Los Angeles is alive.
The city tonight stands outside of everything.
We come to night.
We come to light.
The city is a liar.
May I find my way.
Los Angeles is a dream we cannot bear.
I think of streets black as any river, and beer.
Over loud music a woman calls to her lover.
There is no truth here.
The city is awash with lights.
Even this sacrifice will not save us.
I say *hibiscus* and mean innocence.
I say *guava* and mean childhood.
I say *mosquito netting* and I mean loss.
I say *father* and it means only that.
Happen that we all dream, but the sea is only sea.
Happen that we call upon God but it is only a breeze
ruffling a prayer book in a small church
where benches groan in the heat.
Outside a peacock will not be quiet.
There are so many ways I could undo the night
my father expired if only I could
find the fastenings of time.
Here the green grass is green even with the abundance
of home, even with the weight of exile.
There is a tree in my father's backyard under which

my umbilical is buried. There is no metaphor here.
Bathing on a zinc sheet one night, I sliced my ankle
to bleed my umbilical again.
Look, there is a simple math to loss, to self, to aubergines.
I can sing my father's lineage back half a millennia
but here in Starbucks I struggle with Oprah
to find myself. Which is to say,
I could accept the labels before me,
but only a deeper cut will suffice.
I am not an American, though I want to be.
I am not a Nigerian even though I have the melancholy.
I am something deeper still.
For now, Igbo, a placeholder. Also sometimes,
Druid, on my mother's side. And a red passport.
People say, Christ, if I'd seen what you've seen.
Christ! Mercy! Jesus!
This is my cry, too. I have seen, but I am still lost.
The fog will not part no matter how long I strike
my staff against stone.
There are slavers in my ancestry, slaves too.
Some nights I wake with the bitter of rusty chains
on my tongue, a whip in my hand.
Avatars come and go and come again.
There is only a map fading in the harsh sun.
Some may call me a pessimist, but I am not.
There is nothing gained from loss.
I drink tea in the shade and believe in poetry.
I am a zealot for optimism.

2

Every river is Jordan for the faithful.
They came to the holy mountain by my college.
They climbed for days in their white robes.
They looked like a flock of egrets
resting in the heat and green.
Can a new sky be born?
Nothing I tell you will slake your thirst.
But Pepsi at a baseball game comes close.
If I mourn for all the suffering in the world,
then I have only my ego to blame.
I mourn daily. How can I not?
Let there be love.
There are 20 strings in a Myanmar marionette.
There are 54 ethnic groups in Vietnam.
There are 250 ethnic groups in Nigeria.
There are 100 petals on a blossom of
a Japanese Kikuzakura cherry tree.
Diwali lasts for only 5 days.
Then the lights dim and we forget.

3

In Siena the bells toll to mark the hour.
Outside birds sing. Also scooters whine.
In Nigeria they were ridden by insurance agents
in white shirts. Kids would scream, "American Life Mutual,"
as they kicked up dust in their whiny trail.
As they say in France, *C'est la vie.*
I am like a man climbing a mountain but taking in
none of the view.

I don't know what faith is but
I know this much —
I want to put my fingers in the wounds and swirl them around.
Thomas has nothing on me.
I was seduced as a boy by frankincense
And smoke
And altar lights
And Latin mass
And robes
And wafers and wine
And wooden pews dark with sweat
And confessionals musty with lies
And rosary beads worried for a vision
Then Buddha and the romance of Tibet.
If Zeno's paradox reveals anything it is not that
space and time can be divided into infinity infinitely,
but simply this:
That we can only approximate the object of our desire.
That we are always on a train traveling to happiness.
But what we do reach are coffee, biscotti, and Bob on the iPod.
Alexandria, in Egypt, is both a city and a library —
Hope and destination.
The world is often like this.
Some things look like blood, some
even taste like mud and rust.
They are not blood. They are not.

4

And God stands in disdain as we supplicate.
If love is your nature you will find it.
The frayed carpet and plastic covered chairs
were the stage for my aunt's faith.
Dipping harddough bread into milky sweet tea
she unleashed her anger at the world in prayer.
In another life she could have been a dancer.
In this one, she is a Christian.
In Zimbabwe, Mugabe betrays a people
who make excuses for him.
This is what it is to be a president in Africa.
FUCK YOU HIGH QUALITY—bathroom graffiti, Siena.
In Nazi Germany, a student resistance group called
White Rose. Who knew?
Their slogan: *Wir Schweigen Nicht.*
We, too, will not be silent.
In June and July 1994, O.J. made the cover of *Newsweek.*
By the time the Rwandan genocide made the cover
in August, one million were dead. Four million displaced.

5

Let me know this, too:
The sting of orange zest in my eyes.
And chocolate, decadent and truffled.
And dancing.
And milk fresh and bubbling from a goat.
And the wind holding me as I free-fall from a plane.
And wonder at a goldfish's infinite curiosity.

And cats
and dogs.
And a child's hand brushing my face.
And wings.
And still rain
and still rain.

6

The root of the word *salary* is sal. Salt.
To be paid in salt.
Salt is the weight, salt is the worth, salt is this body.
Say *pepper,* say *amen.*
Some people are necromancers—
They summon repeatedly the body of their pain.
Sometimes I am like that; dissecting the dead.
Sometimes I am merely a practitioner of nostalgia.
Like those heady Nigerian afternoons filled with munching
sugarcane, the molding of fufu for the dip
into stew, fingers fishing for morsels of delight,
the cold slake of coconut water fresh from a nut.
Good fiction is simply the capacity to remember
your life, and yet simultaneously realize
you are inventing every memory.
When I was a child,
South Africa was a story about men
so deep into the despair of a bottle,
dreams dark as the coal they worked.
When I was a child,
vampires lived behind the water tank, skirted
by the modesty of elegant green bamboo.

Now as a man, in the café in Siena, I declare:
Those fucking Germans, those fucking Germans,
so what is my excuse now?

7

It is easy to forget the decadence of glass.
How some of us find it only in fragments.
The glass between us and the world
is often the measure of our wealth.
Looking out at the world through it
colors the hunger beyond.

8

Growing up, Emeka was albino.
How we feared his pink skin and red eyes.
How we loathed him.
To my shame, I never ate with him,
saying: I just ate,
And to my sister under my breath:
He disgusts me.
She never told on me, but made me wait
while she ate with him
—same plate, no utensils—
her eyes never leaving mine.

9

Courage is often invisible:
Old women who buy their own groceries.
Mothers who become shadow.
Women who speak and speak and are not heard
until a man says, Of course, of course.
Children walking through minefields.
Palestinians who don't throw stones,
wanting only food and life for their children.
Palestinians who throw stones,
wanting only food and life for their children.
Israelis who eat in cafés.
People who feed the homeless.
People who don't feed the homeless,
but love their children well.
People who love people.
Who love animals.
Young people who will not be fettered.
Old people who will not die quietly.
Women who dance with wolves.
Women who care for the dying.
People who speak of rage and abuse.
People who suffer pain with a smile.
People who suffer pain loudly.
People who speak up for their beliefs.
Children who protect other children.
Homeless children who smile.
People who have to navigate worlds designed,
consciously or not, to keep them out.
Being black anywhere in the twenty-first century.

10

In Siena, in a beautiful café on Piazza del Campo
drinking coffee while Eastern European refugees beg,
a man says to me: Literature in Italy is not like it is in Nigeria.
There is no suffering here. We have no problems to fight.
The clock on the tower says 4 p.m.
What can be said to a man listening to Bob Marley
on a train speeding through Tuscany?

11

To see the Verrazano Bridge disappear into fog
on a sunny Brooklyn day.

12

Tonight I am waiting, alone,
in my hotel room. I am not waiting
for a lover, imagined or real.
I am waiting for my father.
Which is to say, my dead father.
What I want to understand is overwhelming.
The way a trapdoor in the floor holds nightmare.
I have lost all sense of scale.
The father I wait for is not real.
He is not the man who died five years ago.
And yet he cannot bend into metaphor.
I want to say I love him.
Barthes would say I do:
You do because you are waiting.

The way a plane cuts through clouds.
Like the mandarin waiting for the courtesan for ninety-nine days.
Like Blake setting a place for God.
Like the Red Vines I try to wrap around my rage.
The tender gesture says: ask me anything.

Benediction

1

Let me tell you about sorrow.
A mother wandering down a street calling
for a child while planes scream overhead.
And bullets around her cutting down goats,
and trees and men and women and finally her,
and in the dust, just out of reach of her dead hand,
her son's severed head.
And somewhere, someone is wailing.
Let me tell you about hate.
A bayonet on the end of a rifle run through
a teenager's bony chest by a swarthy soldier
frothing from the pleasure of it, amazed
at the sound of it, flesh sucking on metal.
And this boy dying and
his eyes do not lose their burn,
staring at his killer as though to say,
Do it, do it now because I will do it to you,
and even as I die, I am doing it to you.
Let me tell you about love.
Suheir on a rooftop in Jersey City cries into her cell.
They won't stop coming, she says.
E-mail after e-mail after e-mail.
And in them they are dying, or dead or afraid.
And I can't hold it, can't hold it.
We are talking about Lebanon and Gaza.
In Los Angeles I make soothing sounds,
as I fill the pot for coffee. I wonder
if I will still be able to watch CSI.

2

A cubist way to see the world.
Fractured histories,
at once present and absent.
What is this stone tongue that won't let me
make poetry in Igbo?
Akwa — egg
Akwa — cloth
Akwa — cry
Akwa — bed
Tone is God.
Akwa kwara akwa maka na akwa ya kuwara na akwa.
The cloth cried because its egg broke
on the hardness of the bed.
This is not avant-garde. This is Igbo.
Ehagi bu egu nagu irem.
Your name is a hunger on my tongue.
Enya gi bu ihe na echekwubem.
Your eyes are the light that shelters me.
Omoloma gi but omoloma'm.
Your beauty makes me beautiful.
I bu ndu na edubem.
You are my reason for living.
These words I learned tell me nothing:
faith, god, fire, man, death, sun, wind,
sea, sea, sea.
I learned *dictator* and it meant empty.
I learned *fratricide.*
I learned to hate and the world ground on.
In a bleak time, those who indulge are sybarites.
I am choosing a name for my lover.
Nganga — elegance.

Amara—grace.
Obi—heart.
Ngozi—blessing.
In the old country my mother planted flowers
in the face of my father's disdain.
In every garden,
in every house,
no matter how long
we lived there.
I think it was the war,
the Blitz in England, that took all the flowers.
I think it was for the love she couldn't show him.
I think it was for me.
To show me that only the unspeakable remains.
And remains as gesture.
Eden is not the thing we seek.
It is the thing we cannot find.
It hangs tremulous like a spider's web from a branch.
This is the body of Christ.
Amen.

Histories

1

Boys are taught to kill early.
Five
when I shot a chick in my first ritual.
Eight
when chickens became easy.
Ten
when I killed a goat. I was made to stare
into that goat's eyes before pulling
my knife across its throat.
Amen.
I thought it was to teach me the agony
of the kill. Perhaps it was
to inure me to blood.
To think nothing of the jagged resistance of flesh,
to make the smell of rust and metal and shit familiar.
I have never killed a man, but
I know how, I know I can,
I know that if the timing were right I would.
I am afraid that I might not feel sorry.
I am afraid that I will enjoy it.

2

Joyce and I share the ghosts of mothers
wandering the halls of our novels, calling
for a light that cannot fit there.
It is time for dinner.
Approximate a field tool shorn of wooden handle,
floating above a block of Plexiglas.
Or a comb caught in the transparent mount of a frame.

Everywhere I turn, Africa is dead.
They don't care for our ecstatic, our desire,
they care nothing about us.
We are a dead people. All that matters is how close
we match, or approximate the exhibit.
And over here, Ladies and Gentlemen, beside
the Venus Hottentot, an example of twenty-first century
       African writing.
Note the use of proverbs, puns, and allusions.
Also the landscape of huts and pots curdling on hearths.
Even now angels stalk me in my fear.
One way to know you are in love is to feel
the incompleteness of yourself settle on you
like dust in an abandoned house.
Oh, to be Rilke and to be full of suicidal angels and no fear.
This is the razor's edge.
In the desert, new cartographies are drawn by wind and desire.
Ask the Tuareg why they must and they say: We must.
I want to believe that living things can hear me.
I want trees to nod when I caress their bark,
to shiver in the delight of my touch.
A bird shat on my head. Does that count?
I have killed before. Felt the delight of blood.
The sticky way it coats everything
so that you can't chase the flies from your eyes,
you cannot scratch the itch on your nose.
The way sweat stings reluctant tears.
There is little that will remind you of home more than
the sweet smell of fur singeing in the fire, singeing
as the goat turns slowly, too far to cook
but close enough to burn the fur,
and the knife scraping it off and it sounds
like when you scrape the sticky papaya seeds

from the cutting board, a miracle,
flesh turned wood, and your heart becomes
a stone harder than the mango pit your teeth scour
for one more taste of the sweet,
and it always comes back to that.
Killing begins with the story of land.
My land, and my father's land and
his father's land before him.
Amen.

3

What can you say about growing up in Nigeria?
Does anyone care that you picked plump red and yellow
cashews from trees and ate them in the sun,
the sticky-sweet of them running down your arms.
And later, the seeds collected and roasted for the nut.
And in prison, men writing names on bodies with the sap.
Names to obscure their real selves,
names to protect what might be left over
when they returned to the world from hell.
It is an old trick, to fool death by writing
a new name on your body.
I was afraid my soul would be obscured,
and in cowardly script, almost invisible to the eye,
scrawled with the tip of a needle: Saddam.
It has faded to a nice smudge on my belly,
where a network of hairs and stretch marks
pretend it never happened.
I learned alchemy in prison.
Words mean only what you want them to.
You say *sunshine* and you mean hope.

You say *food* and you mean refuge.
You say *sand* and you mean play.
You say *stone* and you mean, I will never forget.
But you do, but you do and thank God, thank God.
When they called from the university,
in all innocence, they said,
There is a letter for you from *your* president.
They had never heard the words Dele uttered
before that letter bomb exploded.
You tell your friend who runs the place.
And you sit turning the letter over and over,
while she gently clears the wing
and then comes back to sit with you as
you turn the letter over and over.
Fingers ignorantly searching for wires.
Over and over you turn wishing you were American
and could have the naïveté to not fear a letter from
your president. To feel only pride or the gentle rise
of acerbic wit as you prepare
to decline whatever is on offer.
You smile at your friend who has no reason
to be here except she won't let you die alone
and you rip the envelope open.
There is no explosion.
A letter spills out with the crest of the president.
You are crying.
You are glad you are not dead.
You are glad that your country is proud of you.
You are glad to see the day when things can change.
You are confused.
Your friend is holding your hand.
Dear Eloise,
blessing be upon your name.

Is this what it feels like to have your father love you?
To not fear his return?
To not expect to be hit when he reaches for you?
What can it feel like to believe
that the world is inherently good?
Let there be love.
I am not a pessimist.
I believe in love.
It has, however, often been a foreign country to me.
This is the body of Christ.
Sanctificum.

4

When I was five,
I tried to fetch water from the unfinished septic tank
with a plastic teapot for my sister's tea party.
I fell, the weakness of water-eroded wood giving beneath me.
What kind of son betrays his father like this?
As I emerged, I saw he was about to leap.
Maybe that was why he beat me so much.
Maybe it is too much for your father to believe
that he would give his life for you.
And who can blame him?
I wanted to be a son you could be proud of, Father.
I killed the way you taught me.
But I liked dolls and tea and playing with my sister.
Forgive me.
This is the body of man.
Sanctificum.
And then the war followed.

5

But it began in 1660.
Exploited by Portugal and Spain,
under a gentleman's agreement, for slaves
important to the New World, Nigeria,
though unnamed, was ignored by a British Empire
too busy fighting for South Africa and India,
while putting out the fires
of rebellion in America.
But declining fortunes in India,
the need to curtail power of European rivals,
conspired with the Crown's greed to needle
abolitionists to battle.
Wrenched from Spain and Portugal,
we are the prize,
rich in palm oil,
rich in camwood,
rich in gold,
rich in ivory.
Knitting on the upper deck of a steamer
headed north on the Niger, Lady Lugard,
the wife of Britain's governor
for the Niger territories,
had an epiphany:
"Why not call it Nigeria, dear?"
And he did.

6

This is the body of the world.
We believe in duality.
That is our way.
New religions pose no threat to old
gods only too grateful to shirk.
There is no conflict. We understand.
Many gods sew together our fractured selves,
the schizophrenia that is our true human nature.
The taste for fraternal blood can never be sated.
Again and again,
we kill our kinsmen,
rape our mothers,
pillage our fathers,
make whores of our sisters.
Yet the thirst never slakes.
Caught in black-and-white images:
A young girl howling down a Vietnamese road,
napalm peeling skin raw like a summer grape,
mouth rictusing around scream.
The shadow of child holding book
seared into concrete; Nagasaki.
Bodies sponging up tropical rivers, burst
like overripe mangoes in the sun.
And many will hate me when I say,
None of this is worth dying for.
Be sure: your sins will find you out.
Numbers 32:23.
Even as Chaucer dipped quill into ink
and caught a caesura of history in a language
still undecided, the University in Timbuktu
prepared to celebrate its bicentennial,

its scholars capturing epics
that are now lost in the loose shuffle of sand
covering it. Of all the writing and books,
only a fragment of clay tablet was found.
It spells out the message:

I wrote that in another life.
Inshallah.
Hallowed be thy name.

7

As I grow older I want to hold my mother.
Hold her to my chest and soothe her.
Cradle her head that is small, thin as a sparrow's,
and say, He loved you, he did.
All those years, they count for something.
And the only lie would be the not knowing.
And I am a man, too.
And like my father, bad, bad, bad.

8

When you first see a man die
from a machete cut or a bullet,
which is to say, when you first confront
the astonishment of blood and feel it
creep over your skin like a sugary sludge,
even though the cracks it wets are not your skin,
but really the obsidian of the road,
you feel sick in ways you thought not possible.
A deep and wonderful bile
that can never leave your stomach.
And then the days pass and you become familiar
with its ways and it bothers you no more
than cherry syrup dripped over pancakes.
You grow bored and impatient with it all.
With the shock of those just-arriving moments.
After that, people can die around you day and night
and you go on without noticing.
My capacity for it scares me.
Blessed are the undefiled in the way.
There are two ways to view the body.
Resurrection and crucifixion.
Everything that falls between is ritual.

DEAR YUSEF KOMUNYAKAA:

Your poem "Ode to the Drum"
pulled me back from many night terrors.
May I roll it around my lips and not kill it
for its exquisite touch.
May I find a way to beat a song back
into these tired lines, these words.
Amen.

Dew

1

I don't want to wake up in a dark Tanzanian night
without you, or the light of you.
I return to sleep but the smell persists,
the smell that woke me from the deep.
It is a wetness that is dank with earth and leaves
and a compost that can be found nowhere but here.
The funk of my father shaving in the cold
without water or lather and the blade
rasping against cheeks old with denial.
His fingers search for stubble in the dark.
But that smell. It is an old smell.
Somewhere between asparagus piss and towels damp
with the knowledge of snuff washed from hot nostrils.
Somewhere between cloves and the smell of wet grain.
Sometimes it comes upon me now.
Five years after his death and thousands
of miles from where he lived. And died.
It comes upon me, this smell, and I say,
This is my father. This is my father's spirit.
A Montblanc pen and a moleskin notebook.
Some things here are quietly masculine.
Outside an owl hoots. Inside, the kettle whistles.
There is rain on the roof as I resist this fervent impulse
to be didactic. To say, Father, how could you?
There in the forest is the first glimmer of light.
There it is again.
I am not seeing things so much as
things are seeing me.
Consider this.
My grandfather never summoned the dead,
no matter how heartbroken the widow.

Things that are dead are better left dead.
What is most scary is not whether we can see
the ghost but, rather, the moment the ghost sees us.
Tomorrow is lost like this.
There are fewer things sadder than moss
crawling up an airport wall.
Fractals are like this.
You measure and measure but there is no end.
A wound in the heart *can* core the earth.
Still, as far as I know, a straight line is still
the fastest way between two points.
Somewhere I saw a white horse gallop
through a sky as dark as velvet, ripe as an aubergine.
There can be no doubt.
My desire is struggling up the mountain.
My fear is a shower of pebbles.
Your son is trying to be a good man, Mum.
Your son is going to be all right.
There are no names for red.
As for amber, what words can be said to God?
Holy the glow.
Holy the O.
Holy the old.
Amen.

Nomad

1

The glue that bound the pages of an old book dries and breaks free.
I am snowed on by flakes of white. Snowed under.
This book will not let me leave unmarked.
I want to be like the man
in Bolaño's story sitting in
an abandoned car by the highway.
But I don't want to read Sade. No.
I want to read a text so luminous,
so fucking iridescent that it will transform me
into a creature that I have no name for.
But what is it, this excrescence on my soul?
And how is it that a Californian poet could write so eloquently
about this Nigerian boy's life without even knowing him?
Or knowing that the act of faith his words would become
could gather in such a heart from the rain.
And finding him, in the middle of my life,
and tracing the tremulous balance of those words
I say his name over and over—Larry, blessing be upon you.
And eventually he came back from death in my dreams,
smoking a cigarette so raw he picked tobacco from his tongue
and flicked the speck into the light. Through that cloud
with a bushy mustache more Croce, he said,
You will not understand it all. Not now, maybe never.
But I was in a hurry and scribbled those lines for David.
But he was right. Even now as I count the signs
walking by a river in Princeton, it remains occluded:
Two blue jays—the Christ—before and after.
Three snakes—the wisdom of body, heart, and the mind.
Five white-tailed deer—breaking for the trees,
the five mystical wounds that will not heal.
I have always envied the stigmata.

But it is the ordinary things, isn't it?
The daily sigh of the world that defeated Eliot—
And even anger can die in this way.
Until there is nothing but ash on a dinner plate
next to dried gravy and a cold, gray piece of meat.
Like the photos of my dead father.
Skin blacker than worked leather, and wrinkled.
As though all the anger in him had burned out on his skin.
And small as a bony wet cat and I think, How could it all
become so pedestrian, as I step out into traffic.
The bus misses me, but I am tenacious,
there is another at 6:15.
There is a God, I chant, there is a God.
But it is just the apple pie à la mode talking.
I am getting wet, Larry, I am getting wet.
Hey, Rilke, I have finally figured out who your terrible angel is.
And his face is the morning and his laugh is the night.
But I shan't tell on you.
What kind of poet rats out another?
In the Nigeria of my youth, women bleached their skin, leaching
all that was black except what was too stubborn to go,
whorling elbows and knuckles and knees,
and memories blotching faces—
Yellowish-blackish-greenish-blue—
Skin as bruise.
Holy be thy name, O Lady of the mercury soap,
O Lord of the encroaching light.

Renewal

1

Water and sand and the world.
This was my childhood.
And rice steaming under tomato stew heavy with chicken and thyme.
And ice cream melted and coarse to the taste.
And the endless cough of savanna.
And chopper bicycles.
I am speaking of Afikpo.
The slant of the telling and it means according to each man.
The gang or the police.
The bumper car or helicopter.
The killing or the clubbing.
Particular, like the scent of summer light.
I am speaking of Los Angeles.
Holy be the Crips.
Holy be the Bloods.
Holy be the 18th Street.
Holy be the LAPD.
The historical narrative hinges on the sound
of a car cutting the gravel as it turns.
The war is still raging.
The poor keep dying.
Which is to say, young Americans.
Which is to say, young Palestinians.
Which is to say, young Israelis.
Which is to say, young Africans.
It's not that the rich don't care,
but how can the Virgin be set free of the icon?
Marvin sang and sang, but the spell didn't work.
It's still happening, brother.
This is how we suppress the trauma.
The Turks are lying about the Armenian ghosts.

I want to rampage through the world and rectify:
Blood for blood.
Death for death.
What can happen to all this hate?
Where do I bury it?
To exit is the first stage of enlightenment.

2

There are four mothers for the world.
For the joy of this knowledge.
The mother is lost.
Holy the mother.
Holy, holy, holy.
What have we built? As Igbos, what have we built?
Perhaps the greatest bridge to the waking world across dreams,
between what can be imagined and said.
But what use is this if we cannot buy rice?
What good is it if we squander it?
I will follow the Nile one day.
And the Niger, too. Perhaps even the Cross.
Glory be to free-flowing water.
Soon it will be gone and sand
makes a less adequate metaphor,
shifting and erasing the tracks in it.
If I were really a philosopher, I would travel.
My continent awaits me.
Africa is a dream for us all.

3

Have you ever woken to find it *was* you
drinking coffee and looking out all along?
We killed our grandfathers.
Then we killed our fathers.
Now we are killing ourselves.
Next will be the sons.
This is our legacy.
For fear of being loved we will kill the world.
Sometimes a bird slicing sky has no other meaning.
Sometimes water slakes out thirst.
Even this can be enough.

4

My mother left a question mark, an unresolved ellipsis,
an echo maybe of a robin fluttering between gray
gravestones rising like abrupt cliffs in the sea of green.
I am her desire spreading into night like a rude whisper.

Now there is little to mark my days
save the slow steady reliability of water,
and a pump that measures, in perfect cups,
the shallow depths of each falling away
into an endless bucket, like a door opening to shadow,
and the way her heart held it open for me.

5

How foolish of me to keep knocking
on the door to a heart whose face remains closed to me.
All these words, Father, all these words written
searching for you when it was never you, was it?
It was always me.
If I could build you a funeral pyre
I would lay down my hairbrush,
my G.I. Joe,
my books,
my pencils,
my drawings,
my books,
my dreams,
my books,
all.
Then fire.
I set you free that night, Father.
When you came back in that yellow Volkswagen,
in that dream.
I made a boat of honor for you.
Woven of poems and words and not-words.
I set it on the ocean.
Fr. Obuna said to me,
A gift is freely given and a gift
is freely returned.
It has taken me thirty years
to understand this.
Yemaja has your heart now.
May she be merciful.
May she love you.
The wound bleeds no more.

Which is to say,
what I have desired is like salt
left out all night and gone.
Dew be soft.
Dew be salty.

6

Bean.
I feel so alive in you.
Damn the dead.
Damn the dying.
This is a hard light to weave words in.
If men could truly write love letters,
what would we say?
Jesus forgive this stake.
I must drive it home.
Something must die, for us to live.
We still haven't figured out the way.
From the train window,
a lone tree grows out of a pylon.

7

I want to say this:
What is left after the poet's gaze rips into us?
Cadaver?
Body?
Light?
If butterflies could know this melancholy.
This is a terrible, tragic alchemy.

But I will work the metal of my being
until it reflects only what is there.
And can I stand before this pure id?
Before this darkness that can burn the cornea?
Which is to say that there is only light.
Which is to say that there are only angels.
Which is to say that this is not death.
Holy is the hope.
Holy is the desire.
Holy is the awe.
Holy, holy, holy.
Amen.

8

This is not a lamentation, damn it.
This is a love song.
This is a love song.
Like reggae—it all falls on the offbeat.
If there is a way, it is here.
They say you cannot say this in a poem.
That you cannot say *love* and mean anything.
That you cannot say *soul* and approach heaven.
But the sun is no fool, I tell you.
It will rise for nothing less.

ABOUT THE AUTHOR

Chris Abani's prose includes *Song for Night* (Akashic, 2007), *The Virgin of Flames* (Penguin, 2007), *Becoming Abigail* (Akashic, 2006), *GraceLand* (FSG, 2004), and *Masters of the Board* (Delta, 1985). His poetry collections are *Hands Washing Water* (Copper Canyon, 2006), *Dog Woman* (Red Hen, 2004), *Daphne's Lot* (Red Hen, 2003), and *Kalakuta Republic* (Saqi, 2000). He is a professor at the University of California, Riverside, and the recipient of the PEN USA Freedom to Write Award, the Prince Claus Award, a Lannan Literary Fellowship, a California Book Award, a Hurston/Wright Legacy Award, a PEN/Beyond Margins Award, the Hemingway Foundation/PEN Award, and a Guggenheim Fellowship.

The Chinese character for poetry is made up of two parts: "word" and "temple." It also serves as pressmark for Copper Canyon Press.

Since 1972, Copper Canyon Press has fostered the work of emerging, established, and world-renowned poets for an expanding audience. The Press thrives with the generous patronage of readers, writers, booksellers, librarians, teachers, students, and funders—everyone who shares the belief that poetry is vital to language and living.

Major funding has been provided by:

Amazon.com

Anonymous

Beroz Ferrell & The Point, LLC

Cynthia Hartwig and Tom Booster

Golden Lasso, LLC

Lannan Foundation

National Endowment for the Arts

Cynthia Lovelace Sears and Frank Buxton

Washington State Arts Commission

For information and catalogs:

COPPER CANYON PRESS
Post Office Box 271
Port Townsend, Washington 98368
360-385-4925
www.coppercanyonpress.org

Copper Canyon Press gratefully acknowledges Amazon.com
for its extraordinary support for *Sanctificum*.

This book is set in Fedra Serif, a contemporary
typeface designed by Peter Bil'ak. Book design
by Valerie Brewster, Scribe Typography.
Printed on archival-quality paper at
McNaughton & Gunn, Inc.